MARI HEMMING PHOTO: DAN TOBIN SMITH

Translation: Rolli Fölsch and Garry Jones

Albert Bonniers Förlag

Aquavit

According to the dictionary aquavit is vodka flavoured with cumin. Most people call it "brännvin" (distilled wine) instead of its quite ironic name derived from the Latin "aqua vitae", the water of life. This was a term used in the days when liquor was used more for medicinal purposes and not for getting drunk.

This essential ingredient of the smorgasbord is not as Swedish as we like to think. Initially it was the Dutch who produced aquavit, but this was a costly method as they used distilled wine to make it. A more cost-effective way of distilling spirits from grain had been developed by the Russians. This was introduced here during the 16th century when Swedish soldiers returned from victorious campaigns – a rather unique trophy of our wars with Russia, and one that has lasted through the years. In spite of the foreign influence on the origin of its production, saying "skål!" when toasting with vodka is an old Swedish custom. When the Vikings drank their mead, a fermented blend of honey and water, they said "skål" for the glory of their gods and future conquests. "Skål" is an ancient Swedish word for drinking bowl.

Until the end of the 19th century traces of the fusel oil used in production had given vodka a nauseating taste. Attempts to eliminate this had proved fruitless so various spices, herbs and berries had been added to disguise the taste. A Mr L O Smith came up with a way of producing an absolutely pure spirit, "absolut renat brännvin", which made him known as the king of vodka and his portrait is now on the Absolut Vodka bottle. Being not only a smart businessman but also a well-known social reformer, Smith wanted to produce cheap vodka for the poor which would improve their health. Alcoholism was widespread in the lower classes of society but the general belief at the time was that it was the fusel oil rather than the alcohol that was harmful. Although it is no longer necessary people still flavour their vodka with a diversity of additives, of which it is worth naming blackcurrant, wormwood and elderflower. A 16th-century monk's recipe explains how they used to place some herbs into a glass of aqua vitae and let it stand in the sun for three hours. The modern version of this quick-fix infusion is to place the bottle in the dishwasher for a cycle. For anyone mixing their own, a general rule of thumb is to use twice as much spirit as flavourings. After a few days you have a basic mixture to which you can add more vodka according to your preferred strength and flavour. Imagination is the only boundary of tastes you can create. Anyone fancy a shot of garlic vodka?

Blåbär-Blueberry

Ever since the Vasaloppet ski race started in 1922 blueberry soup has been an important feature of the event. The refreshing warm soup is served at various feeding stations along the 90-kilometre route, making it Sweden's, if not the world's, first ever sports drink.

The Vasaloppet has steadily increased in popularity with 119 participants in 1922 to more than 15,000 skiers today. Local women have always taken care of the soup kitchens, even picking all the berries themselves until the number of skiers got too big in the late Fifties. In recent years nutritional sports drinks have become science and the top skiers of today have a range of specialist products to help them. A humorous myth from Vasaloppet is that people finishing last have spent too much time drinking blueberry soup. As a result, these recreational skiers are now referred to as blåbär, a term that has found its way into the Swedish language as a nickname for amateur.

Although it's a serious race, Vasaloppet would not be as popular without the recreational skiers. Statistics say the average participant is a 42-year-old man who has been in the race four times and completes the track in just over eight hours, about twice the time of the winner. The event came about because of an important episode in Swedish history. In the 1520s nobleman Gustav Eriksson Vasa tried to rally support in Mora for an uprising against the 150-year-old Swedish-Danish pact. He was met by scepticism and with the Danes at his heels he fled on skis towards Norway. Terrifying reports then reached Mora of the Stockholm Bloodbath, in which 80 members of the aristocracy had been beheaded upon command of the Danish king. The best local skiers were sent after Gustav Vasa to pledge their support and caught up with him in Sälen. After that the revolt could begin in earnest. The Swedes triumphed and on June 6 1523 Gustav Vasa was elected the first King of the state of Sweden. Many historians have said that the entire episode is a fable. Nonetheless, when the 400th anniversary of Vasa's flight was approaching, a journalist proposed a commemorative ski race along the original route, albeit in the opposite direction. Little did he know that it would become the country's biggest annual sporting event, so popular that some fans would like the race date of the first Sunday in March to be proclaimed Sweden's national day instead of June 6. It is telling that both these important days come from the past of Gustav Vasa.

Classic cars

Classic American cars from the Fifties and Sixties have a peculiar status in Sweden today. Throughout the long winter fanatical owners work on classic Chevrolets and Buicks with the sole aim of showing them off at summer rallies. Surprisingly, Sweden has the world's largest number of well-preserved American cars.

In the Thirties as many as 90% of all cars in Sweden were imported from USA. They were more suited to the rough roads here than Sweden's first own car, the Volvo, launched in 1927. Twenty-five years later the car turned into an affordable status symbol for the young, and Sweden got its very own teddy boys, the raggare. Although the Swedish aerospace company (SAAB) launched a new car after the war, to the raggare these standard family motors did not have the same appeal as the American cruisers which became cult symbols. As crowds of raggare took to the roads, drunken and disorderly behaviour followed them around and they would often besiege entire towns during the summer parties of the Fifties and Sixties. Despite this, many cars remain intact and a real beauty can be worth almost as much as a new car.

The typical fan of today's Fifties nostalgia is a mature man of stable income, who has the potential to realise his adolescent dream, fondly polishing his most prized possession. These cars, now known as Classic Cars, are often in better shape than ever. The favoured models are from 1955 to 1959, preferably a Thunderbird or a Cadillac, but even a Chevy Impala 59 with side wings appeals to the real Classic Car enthusiast. He will tinker with it and wax it through the colder months as these vehicles are for showing off only and totally unpractical for everyday or winter driving. In the summer he will be seen cruising around in his large shiny car. His wife and children may come along, but entrusting them or anyone else with the steering wheel is unthinkable. Todays' cruise-rallies are quieter affairs than in the times when local residents used to barricade themselves behind locked doors. Towns now compete to organise the rallies in which thousands of old cars cruise around a closed-off road in the town centre for half the night, lap after lap after lap. People line the streets, waving at the priest in his Ford Fairline, or the IT genius in his Pontiac. During the rallies one would be forgiven for thinking that one had stepped back into the Fifties as the raggares' dress code is brylcream, winkle-pickers and black leather waistcoats. And let's not forget the furry dice hanging on the rear-view mirror and the obligatory elbow resting on the open window.

Timbered gable, Sundborn

D

Design

In recent years the simplistic and functional concept of Swedish design has seen a revival abroad. But its minimalistic roots can be traced back hundreds of years to a time when Sweden was a country of extreme poverty and a harsh form of Protestantism prevailed.

Meagre times called for practical solutions in the home. The Church also decreed vanity a sin and made ornamentation illegal and for these reasons Sweden was regarded as a country with nothing to offer the world of design. This started to change in the early 1900s when admirers began to recognise and promote the Swedish style. The international breakthrough came in the Thirties, when the American style magazine House and Garden declared "Swedish Modern" as one of the seven most innovative furnishing styles in history, equivalent to Rococo.

Bruno Mathsson became the leading expert on chair design. With his beliefs in healthy and down-to-earth living, he introduced ergonomics into furniture design, often merging the seat and backrest into a single unit.

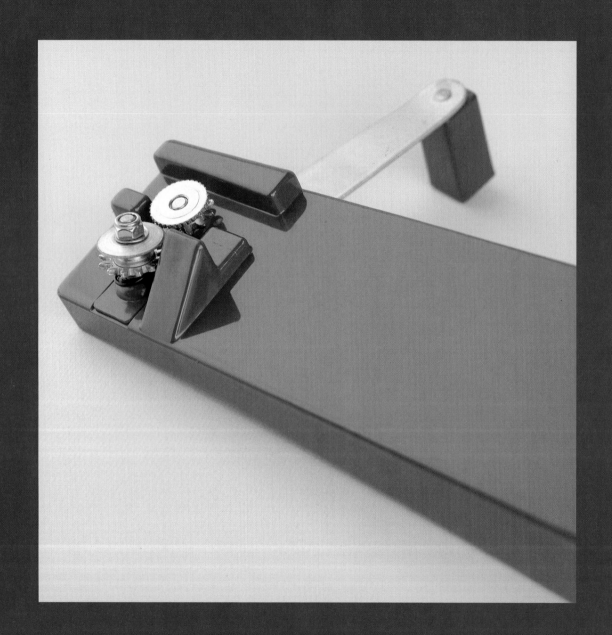

  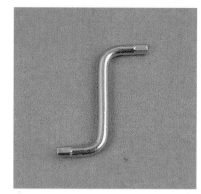

"Scandinavian Design" became an internationally recognised term in the Fifties, with its amazing abundance of forms, renewing everything from furniture to everyday products. Ericofon, the bold telephone nicknamed the Cobra, was declared as one of the century's finest examples of product design by the New York Museum for Modern Art in 1972. A prominent advocate of beautiful household utilities was Sigvard Bernadotte, son of King Gustav Adolf VI. The imaginative and elegant work by the "Design Prince" can be found in almost every Swedish home, such as his greatest success, the tin opener Red Klara. The porcelain industry was revived by Stig Lindberg, whose vivid creations included everything from washbasins to unique stoneware. His dinner service Berså became a favourite of the Swedish people and is still popular today. In 1943, at the age of 17, Ingvar Kamprad founded the Swedish furniture giant IKEA. His winning concept was to sell at low prices, ship by mail order and pack flat for home assembly. Although IKEA is now a global corporation the company remains loyal to its Swedish origins and items like the sofa bed Vingåker and the kitchen cupboard Värde bear the same name world-wide, in China as in the United States.

Emballage-Packaging

Today's packaging often bears sentimental resemblance to the cartons and wrappers of yesteryear. Classic brand names have had their packaging updated, but changes have been small and carefully applied so each item stays immediately recognisable to faithful consumers.

Many families stay loyal to certain brands throughout generations. A good example of this is Bullen's pilsner sausages that were introduced in the Thirties by actor Erik "Bullen" Berglund who had studied the culinary art in Paris. He wrote cookery books for the Swedish man, luring him into the kitchen by presenting cooking in a clear and jovial manner. According to a foreword from one of his books on food, he "liberated the taste of the Swedish man". Bullen's sausages have acquired cult status today and are an essential for aspiring macho men on their adventures in mountains and elsewhere. These hikers say they feel like they have a trusted grandfather in their backpacks when they bring a tin of Bullen's.

Solstickan, "Sun stick" match

The safety match from 1855 is one of the greatest Swedish innovations. In 1936 illustrator Einar Nerman was asked to design a new matchbox for a charity campaign for sick children. Time was short so Nerman took an old image of his son, added a sun and the "Solstickepojken" (literally Sun stick boy) was born.

Pim Pim, Zig Zag, Zoo

These small sweets come in little square boxes that are unique to Scandinavia and very popular in Sweden. Introduced in 1932 Pim Pim is one of the first children's boxes although the brand name is much older, starting off as a sap chewing gum in 1911. The Zig Zag and Zoo boxes are newer, dating from the Fifties and Sixties.

Läkerol

This throat lozenge has been around for 90 years, produced by Ahlgrens who initially ran a rubber factory. At a German exhibition the owner discovered a small chewy tablet made of menthol and liquorice that he copied. Thanks to new ways of marketing in the Thirties Läkerol became an instant world-wide success.

Kalles Kaviar

Kaviar is the classic sandwich paste made from cod roe. Kalle is the fair-haired boy who is on the tube – his father was the managing director at the time of the product's launch in 1954. Abba the manufacturer is a long-established company so Abba the band had to ask permission to use the same name – the reply was a note saying Good Luck and a box of tinned tuna.

MED SÄRSKILT KUNGLIGT TILLSTÅND

KUNG GUSTAF®
LÄTTRÖKT BRISLING
I FINASTE TOMATSÅS

7 311170 061092

Abba Seafood
konsumentkontakt tfn 020-73 20 20.

INGREDIENSER: LÄTTRÖKT BRISLING BEREDD AV SKARPSILL, VATTEN, TOMATPURÉ, FISKOLJA, SALT. VIKT: 106 G, VARAV 74 G BRISLING. HELKONSERV. BÄST FÖRE: DECEMBER 2003. KONTROLLERAD AV ABBA SEAFOODS LABORATORIUM. TILLVERKNINGSLAND: NORGE.

King Gustaf's sardines

This Swedish sardine is better described as a camouflaged sprat. Fittingly the man who gave rise to its name, King Gustaf V, also made use of an alias. He loved tennis and took part in many tournaments under the name of "Mr. G". He played in the Båstad tournament in 1942, at the age of 84.

Grebbestads ansjovis, sprats

It's easy to get confused here but what Swedes call ansjovis is far from the English anchovy. (Those are known as "sardell".) Our ansjovis are sprats – Sprattus Sprattus in Latin. The cans of Grebbestads ansjovis contain a secret mixture of herbs.

Mazetti ögoncacao, Mazetti eye-cocoa

This distinct logo dates from the 1910s when cocoa was sold in loose weight. To differ from the competition Mazetti came up with a bag with printed eyes – "Use your eyes to ensure you get Mazetti's eyes". In the Fifties the logo was brought up to date and will forever be coupled with the nickname "eye-cocoa".

Marabou milk chocolate

Marabou invented the typical, smooth Swedish milk chocolate. The original stork logo was replaced in the Sixties with the company's classic, swirly M, created by Sigvard Bernadotte, Sweden's illustrious designer of royal blood.

Fika

Coffee breaks are the highlight of everyday life, and the more you take the better. A range of "kakor" (biscuits, cakes and pastries) are eaten with the coffee. A famous recipe book for these "kakor", Sju Sorters Kakor, is outsold only by the Bible. Swedes certainly take their fika seriously.

Coffee breaks have been the national pastime for nearly 100 years. In the past the high price often made people choose coffee over more important foods and some even skipped hot meals, a dangerous situation since coffee drinking was widespread among the young. A man destined to win the Nobel Prize, Gustaf Dalén, inventor of the AGA stove, was such a coffee addict at the age of 14 that he developed a coffeemaid in 1883. Being a heavy sleeper, he connected an old wall-clock to a mechanical arm that lit a match 15 minutes before he was due to get up. This, in turn, ignited a petroleum lamp, which cooked a pot of coffee. Young people today increasingly prefer other drinks, but the coffee break remains popular and very much a part of the Swedish national soul.

Oatmeal biscuits

3 dl oatmeal
100 g butter
1,5 dl sugar
1 egg
1 tbsp wheat flour
1 tsp baking powder

Melt butter and pour over the oats.
Add the other ingredients.
Use a teaspoon to place dabs of dough on
a buttered tray. Leave approx 5 cm between dabs.
Bake at 175°C about 5 mins.
Immediately lift biscuits from the tray.
Allow biscuits to cool flat, or "hang" them over a round stick.

Finnish fingers

50 g almonds
5 bitter almonds
450 ml plain flour
100 ml sugar
200 g butter

For brushing:
Egg white
Granulated sugar
Chopped almonds

Blanch, peel and grind almonds but save some
of the sweet almonds for decoration.
Mix all ingredients and chill dough for 30 mins.
Roll dough to lengths, thick as a finger.
Place the lengths close together, brush with egg white
and sprinkle with chopped almonds and granulated sugar.
Cut lengths into 4 cm long pieces. Bake at 175°C for approx. 5 mins.

Cinnamon buns

50 g yeast
150 g butter
0,5 l milk
150 ml sugar
0,5 tsp salt
(1 tsp cardamom, optional)
1,2-1,5 l wheat flour

Filling:
2 tbsp butter
0,5 dl sugar
1 tsp ground cinnamon

For brushing:
egg
(granulated sugar, optional)

Melt butter in a saucepan, pour over milk and warm to 37°C (finger warm). Pour the mixture over the crumbled yeast, add sugar, salt (and cardamom if desired), mix. Add flour, work the dough smooth and allow to rise to double volume. Knead and divide dough in two. Shape into two rounds, 1 cm thick.

Spread dough rounds with butter, dust with cinnamon and sugar.
Roll them up and pinch rolls together at seams.
Cut rolls into rings, 2 cm thick, place rings in paper moulds and let the buns rise.
Brush with beaten egg, sprinkle with granulated sugar if desired, and bake at 250-275°C for 5-7 mins.

Kronans kaka (The Crown's Reward)

It used to be said of state salaries that they were "small but secure". This cake is also small but secure and takes its name from the saying. It serves many and anyone can make it.

150 g almonds
150 g butter
4 dl sugar
4 eggs
200 g boiled, mashed potatoes (cold)

Lemon glaze
200 ml icing sugar
3 tbsp freshly squeezed lemon juice

Butter a mould with detachable sides and sprinkle it with breadcrumbs.
Blanch, peel and grind almonds. Stir butter and sugar roughly together.
Add egg yolks one at a time and stir well. Mix in almonds and mashed potatoes.
Whisk the egg whites to a firm froth and blend them into the mixture.
Spread mixture in the mould. Bake in lower part of the oven at 175°C, for 40-45 mins.
The cake should be slightly sticky. Stir icing sugar and lemon juice and spread on the cake when it has cooled and serve with whipped cream.

Lapponia, Lapland

Glass

Beginning with a little glowing bulb at the end of a tube the magical creation of glass is choreographed by the designer together with the blower. Swedish glass combines the frailty of the material with its bold and daring colours and designs. It is this combination which has created its international reputation.

Swedish glass attracted a sudden and unforeseen attention in the 1910s when pioneers at the Orrefors foundry decided to expand the small glassworks they ran at the company. Simon Gate, an illustrator of bargain books, was hired as a designer and the combination was a hit. Innovative techniques were used and designs such as graal glass saw the light of day. Graal involves blowing patterns into the glass rather than laying colours on top of each other and then processing it to reveal the decoration. The success encouraged other glassworks to pursue their own ideas and the golden age of the Swedish glass industry had begun, an era still going strong today.

It took centuries for glass to be widely used in Sweden. In the 16th century people were advised to aviod it because most banquets at the time ended with all the glass being smashed as part of the entertainment. Not all Swedish glass is created by designers. Sweden turned glass into an everyday item and was the first country to standardise beer bottles. This paved the way for mechanised bottling at the breweries. The bottle standard was established in 1886, coincidentally the same year that Coca-Cola was founded in the USA. Thirty years later the American soft drink company launched a competition for a new bottle design – it wanted a unique shape that would be recognisable in the dark or even smashed into bits. The winning proposal was drawn up by Swedish emigrant Alexander Samuelson whose original idea was based on a cola nut, but he happened to see a picture of a cocoa fruit in an encyclopaedia and presumably mixed the two up. At the time Samuelson worked as a foreman at the Root Glass Company, but he had begun his career at the Surte glass factory, one of Sweden's leading bottle producers, so the world's most famous bottle has its roots in the Swedish glass tradition. The same can be said about the Absolut Vodka bottle. Its shape is based on an old pharmaceutical bottle Absolut's marketing manager noticed in the window of an antique shop, and the final design brilliantly bring together the old and the new.

Haveri-Shipwreck

Remarkably, the greatest blunder of the 17th century is now a national treasure and an important tourist attraction. Foreign visitors to the Vasa Museum are impressed by the size of the ship as was all of Europe when she was being built. If they had only known what would happen to her.

At the time of her construction the Vasa was the world's biggest ever warship. In 1628 Sweden was a super power and the ship's maiden voyage was used as a display of the nation's military superiority. Hoards of spectators lined the shores of Stockholm's islands. Those in charge were probably a bit nervous since a test had raised doubts about the vessel's stability, but they continued with the project because of an undying faith in the tried-and-trusted basic design. But a number of changes had been made in the Vasa and the most dangerous of these was the installation of a large number of canons for a ship of her size. By placing large rocks in the hull they believed they had counterbalanced this top-heavy weight. However, after only a few minutes at sea, disaster struck and the Vasa keeled over and sank.

The tale of the Vasa takes place in two centuries, 300 years apart. Immediately after the catastrophe some objects were rescued from the ship, including 61 of the 64 cannons. The Vasa was then almost forgotten until 1961 when the vessel once again attracted crowds of spectators. After many years of searching, the naval enthusiast Anders Franzén had found the wreck off the island of Beckholmen. During several years of careful preparation, the ship had been moved closer to land and navy divers had blasted out tunnels under the hull in which thick steel cables were drawn, these then being attached to pontoons above. Now, finally, the Vasa was about to break the surface and Swedish television even set up a live outside broadcast unit, a very rare occurrence in those days. Would the hull take the enormous strain? This unbearable tension captured the nation; everyone wanted to witness the outcome. There was not a single television set left in the shops. Workers put down their tools, school children skipped school, one surprised nurse even reported a drop in activity in the maternity ward. The salvage operation was a success, but for the Vasa this just meant the start of a new era – 30 years of restoration work lay ahead. For the first 17 years she was sprayed with a chemical solvent to prevent cracking and several artefacts of high historical and artistic value that had been found with her were put back in place. She was moved once again in 1990 to the specially designed museum on the Stockholm island of Djurgården, to the delight of anyone wanting to experience a unique part of the 17th century.

Ice

The buildings of the Ice Hotel consist of 30,000 tonnes of snow and the furnishings are cut from 10,000 tonnes of ice blocks sawn from the frozen River Torne in Lapland. A fairytale palace of glorious beauty, the hotel is brought to life in the cold months of winter, but is forever destined to end up as a wet puddle when spring arrives.

Initially a small igloo built to house art exhibitions, the hotel developed into a 5,000sq m complex containing a church, an arena, a cinema and even a sauna, all made of ice. You can relax in the "Absolut Ice Bar", one of the most famous bars in the world, which serves "whiskey in the rocks"; all the glasses are made of ice. Here, you can also tempt your taste buds with the icy northern speciality of vodka and lingonberry juice known as Wolf's Paw. All the interior fittings, from the furniture to the chandeliers, are made of ice. First, a chainsaw is used to form a rough outline, then with the aid of water they are shaped to perfection by hand. In the summer nature inevitably takes its toll thawing the hotel, but every autumn it is rebuilt, always in a new guise.

The ice hotel is in Jukkasjärvi, 200 km north of the Arctic Circle, not far from Kiruna. Here, the outside temperature can drop to -40°C, although it is rarely colder than a few degrees below zero inside the ice buildings. Guests sleep in warm sleeping bags between reindeer skins and in the daytime wear thermal clothing even when indoors. Despite Mother Nature's yearly death sentence upon the hotel, summer visitors can experience the cold chill of a Lapland winter in a special version of the "Absolut Ice Bar", located inside a giant refrigerated room. Each autumn, as soon as the temperature is down to -3°C, artificial snow is mixed with water and sprayed onto special steel moulds, some as big as 5-6m. After a few days, the moulds are removed and a new section can be put in place. Jukkasjärvi has an interesting past and in the 16th century it was the last point of civilisation before the harsh wilderness of Lapland. This is where Sami furriers traded goods with merchants from southern Sweden, which is reflected in the name Jukkasjärvi stemming from the Sami word "tjohkki-ras" meaning meeting-place. Today, the traders have been replaced by tourists from all over the world, and visitors to this winter oasis now come looking for exotic adventures with snow and ice.

Pontoon, Marstrand

J

Jakt-Hunt

With 300 000 roaming its forests Sweden has the highest population density of moose in the world. A third of these are killed during the annual hunt but the reproduction is the fastest on the planet and the same amount of moose stalk the forests by the following autumn.

The moose is known as the King of the Forest, a worthy title for Sweden's big game that is the largest land animal in Europe alongside the polar bear. Even if the moose is a fairly timid creature it demands a certain respect. A moose-cow with her calves should never be disturbed, likewise a bull in heat can behave irrationally due to all those hormones. Now and again, there are reports of moose trapping their antlers in clotheslines or in children's swings, which they may mistake for rivals. However, this behaviour could just be an attempt to scrape away some of the woolly coating that covers the horns during spring and summer. This is shed by the mating season when the antlers have to function as sharp weapons in the battles for cows.

The largest moose specimens are found in northern Sweden. The sets of antlers are referred to as crowns and the branches of these known as tynes. Northern moose with magnificent crowns of 26 tynes have been shot, but hunters elsewhere in the country are happy to bag a moose with 12 tynes. The best explanation for the size of the northern bulls is that they feed on lands that are rich in calcium. Irrelevant of their size, most bulls shed their antlers in the autumn and grow a new set in the spring. The idea that the age of the ani-

mal can be determined by counting the number of tynes is pure speculation; there have been instances where two-year-old calves with eight tynes have been felled. Formerly an economic necessity, the moose hunt is now more a matter of lifestyle and keeping an old tradition alive. Hunters often keep the antlers of the animals they kill as a sporting trophy so there is also an element of prestigious competitiveness. Moreover, under an international evaluation system large crowns can be rewarded with gold, silver or bronze

medals. About 250 000 of Sweden's 9 million inhabitants now have a moose-hunting licence and may be able to provide friends and relations with a big, juicy moose steak or two. In non-hunting households this meat is unusual as it is rarely found in the shops. But you can get a taste of the wild by adding a few juniper berries or a shot of gin in the gravy to a simple beef casserole.

Knäckebröd-Crispbread

Swedish crispbread, the noisiest bread ever, has been crunched for 250 years. In the past its long life made things easier for housewives as they only had to bake once or twice a year. Today, people on the look-out for a healthy diet delight in its rich source of fibre.

Before yeast was introduced in the mid-18th century the forerunner to crispbread was so hard that it had to be soaked before it could be chewed. Along came yeast and at the same time the crispbread iron that produces the distinct pattern was introduced. The hole in the middle made for easy storage, as one could slide the bread onto a rod fixed to the kitchen ceiling, out of reach for mice and men. Its lasting qualities were proved in the Forties when a tin containing crispbread was discovered in the Stockholm attic of the Schumacher bakery after the owner's death. This was part of a consignment that had been baked in 1897 exclusively for Andrée the explorer and his North Pole trip in the hot-air balloon Eagle. The ill-fated expedition did not last very long, but the bread in the attic that the baker Schumacher had kept as a memento was still edible after almost 50 years.

Knäckebröd
Recipe for 12 round cakes

50 g yeast
0,5 l lukewarm water
1 l rye flour (or oatmeal)
400-500 ml wheat flour
1 tsp salt

Dissolve yeast in water and add the rest of the ingredients.
Let dough rise for 40 mins.
Roll out as thinly as possible, cut round cakes and place them on a tray.
Prick cakes with a knitting needle, golf peg or similar. Leave to rise for 30 mins.
Bake at minimum 250°C for 3-4 mins, turn the cakes over and bake for another 2-3 mins.

Lapland

This largest and most northern of Sweden's counties is a vast wilderness where one can experience the midnight sun, see the spectacular northern lights and meet nomadic Saami people. Saami is the politically correct term for the people once known as Lapps, a name many of them dislike.

Most maps show two Laplands. There is the administrative county and then there is the vast landmass without fixed borders where the Saami used to roam when they were the only inhabitants of this area. This region is today called Sápmi by the Saami and covers a quarter of Sweden, reaching as far south as Dalarna and also extending far into Norway, Finland and Russia. Reindeer have always been essential in Saami life and being easy to tame they are ideal for drawing the special ackja, sledge. Historically the Saami were hunters who sold reindeer skins and other animal hides to merchants from the south. When profits receded in the 17th century they began to breed reindeer in herds on a large scale. The animals are still reared primarily for their meat although the skin and bones are made into footwear, clothing and other utensils. These items are then decorated in the colourful and intricate Saami patterns.

Saami culture is based on the relationship between nature and humans. The religious leader, or shaman, was the only person that could decipher the will of the gods through drumbeats on a sacred drum. The gods, like the god of hunting and the god of the wind, were said to actually be inside the drum. The bear was a sacred animal so the hunting and slaughter of this creature followed special rituals, dictating that men and women ate different joints of the meat and that the bones be buried according to a particular pattern in special graves. At birth Saami were each allocated a "jojk", a style of singing related to American Indian songs which were used to express feelings or calm the herds of reindeer. The Saami language which is spoken throughout Sápmi belongs to the Finno-Ugric family of languages which also incorporates Finnish, Estonian and Hungarian. There was a time when all Saami lived a nomadic life and followed the herds to their seasonal grazing pastures, but nowadays most of Sweden's 20 000 Saami live a more modern lifestyle integrated in society. But the traditions of the forefathers are kept alive by some of the 2 500 that are still involved in the reindeer trade. This is true especially for those who live a semi-nomadic existence in different houses according to the time of year, depending on the grazing season of the reindeer, and those who stay in traditional tents, kåtor, during the calf branding in July.

The Ice Hotel, Jukkasjärvi

Mother's Meatballs

When asked what he would like for dinner chances are the average Swedish man will answer "Mother's meatballs", traditionally served with lingonberries. The berry contains a natural preservative and has enriched Swedish meals since before the days of refrigeration.

Although meatballs have a firmly established past in Sweden the prefix "Mother's" dates from 1959. It arose in from the world heavyweight fight in the USA between Ingemar Johansson (challenger) and American Floyd Patterson (champion). During the build-up to the match it emerged from the Swede's camp that his entire family were with him and that his mother was doing his cooking. Because of this and because Johansson was often seen out in the Manhattan nightlife, the Swede's unexpected victory caused a big, world-wide sensation, but his mother's meatballs received almost the same attention and it was even suggested that they provided the power for that celebrated right hook. The secret of Mother Ebba's recipe? "Lots of onion," according to the champion himself.

Classic meatballs

400 g minced meat
1/2 onion
150 ml milk or cream
1 egg
5 tbsp breadcrumbs
1-2 tsp salt
1-2 pinches allspice (alternatively cayenne pepper, Dijon mustard or similar)
Butter and/or oil for frying

Mix milk or cream, breadcrumbs and spices and leave to soak for at least 10 mins.
Peel onion and chop finely, brown on low heat. Mix all ingredients.
Roll into small balls (works best with wet hands) and fry.
First brown to seal, then lower heat and fry the meatballs in another saucepan
or in a roasting dish in the oven.

Nobel

Alfred Nobel developed his passion for noisy, sparkling chemical experiments as a child and his love of explosives bore fruit when he invented dynamite at the age of 33. The sparkler adorning the ice cream at the annual Nobel banquet probably has him smiling in his grave.

Although Alfred Nobel (1833-1896) was a hugely successful businessman he lived the life of a gloomy recluse and became so totally addicted to his work that he had a breakdown at 43. He detested fame but instigated the prizes of literature, science, economy and peace that bear his name. It's ironic that Nobel is the most renowned Swede of all time and will forever remain in the international limelight that he wanted so much to avoid. He grew up with his Swedish family in Russia but started travelling the world in his teens, gathering a lot of valuable experience. He became a globetrotter and started various chemical laboratories around the world. He considered himself a cosmopolitan and when drafting his will he decreed that the Nobel Prize be an international award and not a Swedish one. The first prize was presented in 1901.

Though his name is synonymous with the festive banquet held in honour of the Nobel prizes each year one can wonder if Alfred Nobel was ever happy in his private life. The genius who invented dynamite and created a global corporation before he turned 40 paid a high price for his success. In his youth he wrote poetry and he returned to literature later in life for comfort, composing a number of novels including a tragedy entitled Nemesis, which he published at his own expense.

But his talents as an author were questionable and, after his death, his family purchased all but three copies of the book. Seen as an awkward figure in social circles Nobel thrived on portraying himself as an ill-tempered man who kept at a distance. His own contribution to his brother's chronicle of the family includes: "Greatest asset – clean fingernails. Greatest deficiencies – lack of family, unhappy, stomach problems". His former secretary Bertha von Suttner became his

dearest friend and they corresponded for many years. The Austrian woman was a peace advocate who impressed her friend with her outspoken criticism of the military use of dynamite and fittingly she was honoured with the Nobel Peace Prize in 1905. There is a certain logic that the factory in Vinterviken in Stockholm where Nobel carried out his experiments is now a peaceful recreational area with a sculpture gallery.

Opera

Few countries have produced as many opera singers as Sweden throughout the years. The impact of two 19th-century stars is still noticeable as Kristina Nilsson is portrayed as Christine in The Phantom of the Opera and Jenny Lind has been honoured with her portrait on a Swedish banknote.

The most dramatic figure in Swedish opera is King Gustav III, who alongside his royal duties was an avid fan, a theatre director and an actor. He became the victim of a conspiracy and was assassinated during a masquerade ball held at the Stockholm Opera house in 1792. Verdi's Un Ballo in Maschera – A Masked Ball is based on the incident so one can ask if the King's demise, although tragic and untimely, was perhaps one he would have chosen for himself. He often frequented the first opera house in Sweden, the Drottingholm Palace Theatre, which used a remarkably high level of advanced technology for those days. It proved durable too, because it now boasts the world's oldest working stage machinery that booms out rolls of thunder just as menacing as it did in the King's day when the audience was reserved for members of the royal family and their guests. The audience today consists of opera fans from all walks of life.

Polska

The Swedish version of the blues but with a fiery rhythm, the polska contains a magical spirit. Its ancient melodies are linked to myths and legends. It is the music to which the trolls dance deep in the forest, and the sound used by the naked elf as he plays his violin, luring young virgins to their fate.

Unlike the polka, which is defined by its two beats to the bar and a basic pattern of hop-step-close-step, the polska is triple-time like the waltz. The music of Strauss and co. has an emphasis on the first tick, but the national rhythm of Sweden mysteriously stresses the first and third beats in a complex, undefined way. Foreigners often find it a hopeless task to play or dance the polska while Swedes will find it easier having been brought up on polskas like the Christmas song It's Yuletide Again. Benny Andersson from Abba explored the polska's more primitive sides in his Macho Polska that he composed as a solo artist after the supergroup dissolved. He then returned to his musical roots and the folk music that his grandfather had taught him to play on the accordion.

A vital part of the Swedish traditional dress are the garter tassels on the men's socks which have become symbols of the tradition of bearing folk costumes and dancing the polska today. The garters to which they are attached date from the Middle Ages when men wore long stockings that reached up to the thigh inside their trousers. This was before the days of elastics so the ribbons were tied in a peculiar manner on the outside just below the knee of the trouser and the ends were formed into a pompon-like tassel. There are now other methods of holding socks up, but for decorative reasons the garter tassels remain on the folk costumes that stay loyal to their roots and which have themselves an interesting role in Sweden. In the 1880s a wave of nationalistic pride swept the country and the old costumes were revived and modified. Today many villages have their own designs that are often worn at weddings and on other special occasions. In today's high-tech, fast-moving society some futurists sneer at this old tradition, even suggesting that "garter-tassel sentimentality" can prevent progress. These feelings have no place at the annual Nobel banquet where the greatest minds in the world gather at the season's most prominent party. Among the evening gowns and the tuxedos, in the midst of the glitter and the glamour, one will always spot an array of traditional folk costumes being worn with pride and passion.

The Old Town, Stockholm

Q-rbits

Call it artistic licence. This richly decorated floral motif is actually spelt with a K but as the pattern itself is a fantasy creation we took some liberties with the name. From a botanical viewpoint the kurbits paintings should depict only cabbages, but as it stands the lush blooms have become the instantly recognisable sign of Dalecarlia.

The kurbits-painted Dalecarlian horses sculpted from wood, dalahästar, can be found all over the planet in the homes of people who have either been in Sweden or know someone who has. Dating from the 18th century, the distinct kurbits pattern has a basic design of a twisting plant with symmetrical leaves. However, it was up to each local artist to paint the flowers in their own personal style, which could vary wildly. Every village had their own specialists who painted kurbits on furniture, walls and ceilings and everywhere else there was a bit of blank space.

In Dalecarlia, the birthplace of the wooden horse tradition, this style of painting is still alive and kicking, and you can find it on virtually any object under the sun, from clogs to letterboxes and even long-distance lorries.

Elvis Presley once received a dalahäst from his Swedish fans and another was presented to former president Bill Clinton by the Swedish prime minister during an official visit. The making of the wooden horses began a long time ago when lumberjacks worked miles from home and relieved boredom in the evenings by carving wooden horses for their children. The popularity of the models grew and they became a form of currency that travellers could use for food and lodging. Around Lake Siljan in Dalecarlia these horses were painted in the kurbits style and the national emblem of Sweden was born. International recognition was attained at the 1939 World Fair in New York where a three-metre tall dalahäst horse stole the show, creating a demand for 20 000 regular-size models to be shipped over from Sweden. These horses are still made in the workshops of Nusnäs where everything from the carving to the painting is carried out by hand. The diversity of kurbits style means that no two examples are exactly the same and the skilled painters claim to be able to spot their own work. Traditionally, the basic colour of the dalahäst is a reddish-orange, but they also come in blue, white, black and even minimalistic and undecorated variations today. But there is no doubt that it is the kurbits pattern that has made the dalahäst the most Swedish of souvenirs.

R

Red

The red-painted houses dotted around the landscape add a hint of romance and nostalgia but in 17th-century Sweden they were signs of wealth and status. The landowners wanted mansions built out of bricks like European gentry folk, but had to satisfy themselves with red-painted wooden structures as bricks were rare.

The use of red paint spread and for certain types of buildings, like barns and old cottages, this is the only colour a Swede will use. Even barns built with modern construction methods out of sheet metal are often painted red. The original red paint comes from Falun and is based on a unique pigment that is a by-product of copper mining. Falun Red Paint "Falu Rödfärg" is made from a powder extracted from the used copper ore that has been left to mature for at least 100 years. After it is sifted, washed and fired it can be used and the resulting red paint has a truly unique tint which cannot be produced any other way.

Since the 17th century Falun Red Paint has been used on a great variety of wooden buildings and structures – everything from castles, churches and outside toilets have been covered with the distinct, yet somewhat discreet colour. Although the copper mines of Falun have been closed since 1992 the piles of copper ore are big enough for many centuries of paint production. Actually, the dust is a golden brown in its natural state and obtains its redness according to the temperature – the hotter the oven the browner the colour. The paint factory is all that is left from the glorious days of the Falun copper mine that was run by Stora, the world's oldest surviving company until they lost the distinction by merging with Enso a few years ago. No one knows exactly when copper was first mined in Falun, but there is evidence of the mines being in use at the end of the Viking age 1 000 years ago. The world's oldest known business transaction is probably the purchase of one eighth of Stora's Falun Copper mine in 1288 by Peter the Bishop who paid with "two farms with adjoining meadows and fishing waters". Two thirds of European copper was extracted here in the 17th century and the mine was the backbone of the Swedish economy during its heyday. By the time the mine shut for good it had produced over 30 million tonnes of copper stone in its long history.

Falu Red Paint seems to undergo a renaissance at the start of every new century. When Sweden was hit by a nationalistic wave 100 years ago there was a sudden desire to paint all wooden buildings in the enchanting red colour. The paint's current revival has more to do with environmental friendliness than anything else as it is a safe natural product consisting, apart from the pigment, of linseed oil, flour and water. One final important ingredient in this non-toxic magical formula is an iron sulphate, which protects wood and is known to have existed in large quantities in the mine. In 1719 a dead body was found in a mineshaft and produced a mystery as nobody knew who it was. Not until an old woman turned up and identified the man as her fiancée, one Fet-Mats Israelsson, who had been missing for 40 years. It must have spooked her as he didn't look a day older, the iron sulphate having kept his body intact. The remains of Fet-Mats were put on show and he became a bit of a tourist attraction, even gaining notoriety abroad as his destiny was turned into an Austrian opera. After 200 years of posthumous fame, Fet-Mats finally found peace and now rests in a Falun graveyard.

Smörgåsbord

Smorgasbord is one of the few Swedish words and customs to have found its way into dictionaries and restaurants in other countries. The expression is a combination of the Swedish for sandwich and table, a good description as the buffet was initially a table of sandwiches offered with an aperitif.

Upon arrival to 18th-century parties the ladies went off to smarten themselves up after the long journey. In the meantime the men were treated to vast quantities of aquavit by the host who also laid out a selection of crispbread, cheeses and pickled herrings on a table so they could have a nibble while they were waiting. This has evolved into the grandiose feast that we are now accustomed to and for which smorgasbord etiquette is essential. The buffet should be visited at least five times, starting with pickled herrings, followed by a variety of salmon dishes. The third plateful is with cold meat and salads after which come the meatballs and sausages. The magnificent meal is rounded off with fruit and cakes.

A centrepiece on the smorgasbord is the raw spiced salmon, gravad lax. The translation, buried salmon, could sound off-putting but simply dates from medieval times when the fish was stored in pits. Today it is prepared by adding salt and sugar and placing it under a heavy weight for a few days.

Gravad lax

1 kg salmon, mid-section
4 tbsp sugar
3-4 tbsp coarse salt
2 tbsp coarsely ground pepper
2 bouquets of dill
a few coriander seeds (optional)
2 tsp cognac (optional)

Hovmästarsås ("Head Waiter's Sauce")

A necessity for gravad lax and smoked salmon.

Mix:
2 tbsp mustard
2 tbsp sugar
2 tbsp wine vinegar
10 tbsp vegetable or olive oil
2 tbsp finely chopped dill

Fillet the salmon leaving the skin on. Mix sugar, salt and spices. Rub the mixture (and cognac, if desired) into the salmon. Cut fresh dill over the fish. Place the sides together with the skin facing outward. Wrap in foil or place in plastic bag. Refrigerate. Cover with a chopping board and place a weight on top. Turn the salmon frequently. The gravad lax is ready after two days. Scrape off spices and slice fish diagonally.

Rock-carving, Tanumshede

Traditions

By having more public holidays and festivites than most other nations in the world, the calendar reflects the Swedish passion for tradition. New ways to celebrate might be introduced, but the basic components such as food and decorations remain the same – something which the shops are always eager to point out in ads and window displays.

Dead spots in the calendar between holidays are sometimes plugged with foreign customs. Until a few years ago Swedish Halloween was only about honouring deceased friends and family but is now accompanied by the American version with ghouls and ghosts. These foreign influences have upset some traditionalists, but even they accept that international festive variations have now all but replaced the original ones. Sweden's Father Christmas, for instance, used to be a grumpy grey gnome with goats before being replaced with the round, jolly white-bearded figure and his reindeer. Ironically, the figure of today's Santa Claus was drawn up by Swedish emigrant Haddon Sundholm as part of the 1931 Coca-Cola ad campaign. However, most traditions remain true to their roots and the most Swedish of all is Midsummer.

Midsummer

This festivity at the end of June can be traced back to pagan times when the bright nights and healthy growing crops were celebrated by offering floral decorations to Freya, the Nordic goddess of fertility. Today twines of birch and wild flowers are used to dress up the Maypole, a tall, cross-shaped pole the Swedes dance around to traditional songs. Everything from car bumpers to doorways get decorated with an abundance of greenery, while all the young girls comb the meadows looking for seven different flowers to put under their pillows – it is said that their future husbands will appear in their Midsummer night's dream.

Ladies Week

Saint's days stem from Catholicism where each day belongs to a particular saint. Swedes today are Protestants but the calendar still honours a couple of different names every day, 615 names altogether – some of them saints, but also there are also old Viking names. Although masculine names are in majority, the six-day period beginning July 19 consists of feminine names: Sara, Margareta, Johanna, Magdalena, Emma and Kristina. Most Swedes commemorate their name's days with a special cake, which probably has to be eaten indoors during "ladies week" as it is said to be the rainiest of the summer.

Crayfish

Although available all year round the official crayfish season begins in August and is marked by parties that are a bizarre sight for foreigners. Upstanding members of society put on funny hats and bibs, use their fingers to dive into plates of crayfish cooked in dill before slurping and sucking their way through the feast. All this is accompanied by loud singing of snaps songs. These shocking manners resemble those of the aristocracy back in the 16th century when the tradition of crayfish eating began.

Semla

During Sweden's Catholic days, Lent, the period of fasting that covers the 40 days leading up to Easter, was strictly observed. On Shrove Tuesday, the day before Lent, when people needed to fill up on their fat reserves they ate semla, a bun filled with almond paste. Since the Twenties semlas are eaten with whipped cream. As innocent as a bun can be this is the one that killed a monarch, when in 1771 King Adolf Fredrik died of a seizure having eaten too many semla after a large meal.

Semla

50 g yeast
100 g butter or margarine at room temperature
3 dl milk
3/4 dl sugar
1 tsp salt
approx 10 dl flour
cardamom, optional

To garnish:
almond paste, whipped cream and icing sugar

Make the semlas following the recipe on page 33. Split them in half and remove some of the soft bread in the bottom (to add to the almond paste). Place almond paste in the indentation, add a big dollop of whipped cream, replace the top half and dust with icing sugar.

Almond paste

150-200 g almonds
2-2,5 dl icing sugar
soft bread from the semla
1,5 dl milk
splash of double cream

Blanche and grind the almonds. Mix with the sugar. Blend the semla bread with milk, mix in with the almond paste. Add a little cream if required.

Advent and Lucia

The long, dark winter nights often feel bleak and depressive. Then on the first Sunday of Advent the Swedish soul is lit up together with the first of four special candles. The other three are lit on the remaining Sundays in Advent, counting down the weeks before Christmas. Other ways of brightening up the darkness includes drinking hot glögg, and eating pepparkakor. Glögg is a mulled wine with fragrant spices which is served with raisins and almonds. Pepparkakor are thin gingerbread biscuits that have been eaten since the 14th century, making it Sweden's oldest. They are said to make the eater kind-hearted, which could be because they contain ginger and cinnamon, spices that are good for the stomach. On December 13 Lucia processions all over Sweden headed by a local beauty light up the gloomy early morning. The Lucia herself will be dressed in a white robe with a crown of candles in her hair and be accompanied by her maids. As they parade slowly into offices, schools and old folks' homes they spread light, warmth and song. This night was once considered the darkest of the year when people had to protect themselves against evil forces. In the Middle Ages young men went around offering alcoholic beverages for a penny to keep spirits high. The Lucia tradition was introduced in the 18th century and comes from the story of the Catholic saint from Syracuse who died on the burning stakes in the year 304.

Ginger biscuits

Makes approx 150
300 g butter or margarine
4 dl sugar
1 dl maple syrup
1,5 dl water
1 tbsp ginger
1 tbsp cinnamon
1 tbsp ground cloves
2 tsp bicarbonate of soda
12 dl flour

Mix fat, sugar and syrup until soft with a mixer or electric whisk. Add water, spices and bicarbonate and mix in the flour thoroughly. Cover with aluminium foil and let the dough rest in a cool place for at least 24 hours. Roll out the dough thinly, and use cutters to create the biscuits. Bake in 200-225°C for 5 minutes. Let the biscuits cool on the baking tray.

Lussekatter

Use the basic recipe for cinnamon buns (see Fika). Add 10 g of saffron in the milk, but leave out the filling. Roll out the dough with a baking pin, cut it in 10 cm strips and curl them into an S-shape. Press a raisin into both swirls at the ends.

Glögg

1 bottle red wine
1 dl brandy or vodka
5 whole cloves
5 pieces of cinnamon bark
5 peeled, whole cardamoms
1 piece whole ginger
1 pickled orange peel
2 dl sugar

Place all spices in a sealed container, add the spirit and leave for 24 hours. Drain and remove the spices. Heat gently together with the wine and sugar in a pot, but do not bring to the boil. Serve the glögg warm with blanched almonds and raisins.

Uppfinningar-Inventions

Historically most Swedish inventions were discovered by immigrants who brought technical expertise with them from their native countries like Belgium, Scotland, Germany and Holland. But at the turn of the 18th century, Swedish inventors took over and lay the foundations for that respected label: "Made in Sweden".

There are many Swedish inventions that people use in everyday life all around the world. To name a few, John Ericsson's ship propeller, Jonas Wenström's alternating current and Carl Munters and Baltzar von Platen's refrigerator. Recently the medicine Losec has taken away the pain from troubled stomachs all over the world. Some ingenious objects that we take for granted have also seen the light of day in Sweden. One of these is the zip fastener which was the 1913 discovery of Gideon Sundbäck whose idea caught on in a big way when the US army used it to replace uniform buttons and lacing during the First World War. Since then the zip has gone from strength to strength and is today even used in abdomen surgery on people who need more than one operation.

In the 18th century the mathematician Anders Celsius introduced a scale for measuring temperature where water boiled at 0° and froze at 100°. This became the centigrade scale when it was turned around, probably by the botanist Carl Linnaeus, (a.k.a. Carl von Linné), who is famous for placing plants into family groups and giving them latin names. The self-aligning ball-bearing was invented by Swedish textile factory engineer Sven Wingquist, whose idea revolutionised the use of the bearing ball since it removed friction which created problems in the machinery. The product became so successful that he was able to found the SKF company who are now world-leaders in this area and still make ball-bearings for everything from cars to hard disks. In 1952 packaging king Ruben Rausing had an idea for a milk carton in the shape of a pyramid, a tetrahedron. In the Sixties his Tetra Pak company introduced the standard milk carton we all know today.

Another product used by millions around the globe came from Håkan Lans who devised a pointer tool for his work of entering seismic curves into computers during the early Seventies, later allowing Houston Instruments to manufacture and market the product under license. There was an American patent for a similar thing, which was never produced, so every time you grab your computer mouse you put your hand on yet another Swedish invention.

Vikings

The Viking reign of terror that ruled Europe for 300 years is a mixture of myths and truth. The popular image of them as barbarians with horned helmets is not really true, since their helmets never had horns, and they were also respected traders and travellers. But there is no doubt that they were wild warriors.

Up until the middle of the 11th century the Vikings were the masters of the sea. Due to a broad, flat keel their fast boats were able to manoeuvre close to land and to travel a long way up rivers, making it possible for them to land large numbers of invaders in a short time. This gave them the chance to surprise unsuspecting towns and villages when they decided to plunder, which happened quite often. Some of the Viking travels are remembered on numerous impressive rune stones found around Lake Mälaren. One such stone is now standing in the middle of Arlanda airport in Stockholm where it reminds us of these rough travellers from the past.

In their sturdy boats, the Vikings travelled the known trade routes as well as venturing into uncharted waters. Through the rivers of Russia they reached as far as Baghdad where they traded with honey, animal hides and above all slaves. The Imperial Guard in Constantinople was full of Norsemen whose terrifying appearance made them ideal to scare off intruders to the palace. It is easy to picture a Viking on duty with his long hair, ruby earring and grim dragon heads on his shirt together with his large double-headed axe. In the west the Viking Empire included much of England and probably even part of Canada. During a storm the Viking Leif Eriksson who was on route to Greenland came off course and beached at a place he called Vinland which is now known as L' Anse aux Meadows, in Newfoundland. Some think "Vin" refers to grass but Adam of Bremen's chronicle from 1070 tells of Norsemen claiming to have seen wine plants growing wild on an island in the west. There is evidence of Nordic-style buildings at the site so many historians are convinced that Leif Eriksson discovered North America 500 years before Columbus. Even if Leif Eriksson's name for America didn't last very long there is still a Viking connection to the most famous American city of today. When the English settlers renamed New Amsterdam, they replaced the second word with the name of their home town. This town itself was once the centre of Viking power in northern England when it was known as Jorvik, meaning "Horse Bay". It is better known today as York.

Crops, Skåne

X-the unexplained

The extraordinary monster "Storsjöodjuret" of Lake Storsjön in Jämtland looks so much like the Loch Ness monster that some people actually think there is a deep tunnel connecting the waters. A parson became the first person to see the monster in the 17th century and since then there have been many sightings.

In 1949 a pilot saw, from his plane 100 metres up in the air, what he called "a three metre long snake-like creature with three humps" and although there have been many other descriptions of the monster this is the most consistent. In the 1890s King Oscar II sponsored one of the many attempts to catch the beast, however these fishing trips are no longer permitted since the Jämtland County Council has officially recognised the animal as an endangered species and protects it. As with Nessie there is a great deal of scepticism about the monster and doubters maintain there is no proof that the monster has ever existed. But if that is true, then what is in the glass jar in the local museum, where supposedly a monster embryo from 1895 is preserved?

Kristineberg

On November 29, 1946 the day shift in the Kristineberg mine in Lapland had just begun when a miner walked into a blast area. Through the settling dust he saw a shining white figure appear on the rock face, a three-metre high image of Jesus. The news spread like wildfire, pilgrims came to the mine and a photograph was even published in Life magazine. The figure disappeared after two weeks under dirt and smoke from the mine, but an underground church has been built with the repainted image behind the altar.

Dalhalla

In the town of Rättvik by Lake Siljan lies one of the world's most unusual stages, Dalhalla. The amphitheatre got its impressive acoustics from a meteorite that smashed into Earth 360 million years ago. At the time of the strike Sweden was located just south of the Equator and had risen from the tropical seabed. Various layers of dead creatures from the seabed had been transformed into limestone and these layers were turned upright by the rock that smashed into the Earth at 100,000 km/h. Normally the fossil layers in limestone are horizontal, but thanks to the meteorite, Dalhalla has got unique vertical stripes in lovely colours that can be seen in the old quarry wall. Apart from the many music lovers who attend the concerts during the summer other visitors include geologists on fossil hunts, since the area is full of trilobites and other remnants from pre-historic times.

Yta-Space

Sweden is sparsely populated with a density of just 22 people per square kilometre and this in a country with a land mass the size of California. When you compare this with Great Britain's 241 or Japan's 337 you can see why the Swedes' close relationship with nature is part of the national soul.

The Swedish landscape is dominated by mountains, lakes and forest. In the north the mountains form dramatic shapes that roll away smoothly towards the south. Forests cover half of the country and the birch has staked its claim as the national tree of Sweden, being the first tree to take up root here after the Ice Age. In fact the birch grows right up to the tree line, that natural border that marks the highest point of vegetation in the mountainous areas. Thanks to the "Right of Public Access" everyone can walk freely in the Swedish countryside and pick berries, mushrooms or flowers as long as they are not protected species. One does not need the land owners permission to walk across private land as long as one doesn't disturb or destroy the flora and fauna.

You are never far from water in Sweden as there are 100 000 lakes and the coast-line measures 7 000 km. The Stockholm archipelago's 30 000 islands form one of the world's largest and its green, wooded islands stand in direct contrast to the bare cliffs and rocks of the West Coast islands. These were formed when the polar ice cap stripped back the earth creating the smooth rock underneath. Here, only the larger islands have soil, a fact the parson on the small Käringön island decided to do something about. He ordered parishioners to bring a bucket of earth back every time they visited the neighbouring island of Orust. They did, and the parson eventually got a garden at the vicarage. The polar ice cap also left its mark on other parts of the Swedish landscape as it pulled back. The huge amounts of water from the melting ice seeped down into the bottom layers of the ice, creating tunnels which eventually became full of gravel and stone. The result can be seen today in the form of various ridges that appear out of the ground in many places. The flattened peaks of the mountain range in the north-west can also be attributed to the Ice Age when they were rounded off. That's why there are no peaks as high as the Alps, apart from Sweden's highest mountain, Kebnekaise, which rises to 2 111m above sea-level.

Zzz

The great contrast between summer and winter plays games with the Swedes' natural body clock and sleeping hours. Being one of the nations closest to the Arctic and furthest from the Equator means in northern Sweden there is light 24 hours a day in the summer and constant darkness in the winter.

Every year on December 21, the winter solstice, the Swedes start to look forward to brighter days. Stockholm's few hours of daylight in December are envied further north where even the most promising dawn transforms into a murky dusk. At the same latitude as the northern tip of Newfoundland the Swedish capital is one of the world's darkest. Some claim to find the dark comforting and cosy while others become lethargic, suffering from winter depression. When the eye's retina does not absorb enough light the brain produces higher doses of melatonin, the hormone that makes you sleepy. This lack of light is blamed for the constant winter tiredness experienced by 20% of the population, but there is hope in light therapy which is becoming very popular. And the sweet Swedish summer nights more than make up for those dark months.

Although the summer is so short in northern Sweden the long hours of light mean nature catches up with itself. The crops and other plant life catches up with the rest of Sweden after a slow start in only a week or two. The Midnight Sun attracts many tourists, but ironically they have to sleep in hotels with blackout curtains. Even Swedes who have a problem with the eternal light have been known to move their beds into dark cellars to get some sleep. However, foreign photographers and artists love the light and have created some great works of art during the exotic everlasting twilight they refer to as the "Blue Hours". Maybe it is because of the extreme amount of daylight that, despite the shortness of it, Swedes make more of their summer than people do in more southern countries. The entire nation eagerly awaits the next weather forecast on the television, and there is an outrage if the meteorologists promise sun and it rains. If it has been a rainy summer a depression sweeps the country, with the number of divorces filed in autumn increasing with every grey day. Therefore any high pressure is welcomed with that most Swedish of gestures, an upturned face gazing into the sun, putting smiles on the peoples' faces that lasts well into those long, light summer nights.

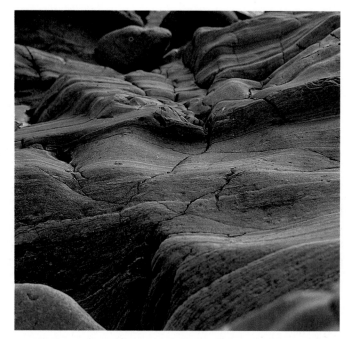

Archipelago, Stockholm

ÅÄÖ

These are the letters that give the Swedish language its exotic look. In simple terms you might say that the dots are there to make pronunciation easier, separating different sounds. Nowhere else will you find all three letters in an alphabet, although Å is found in other Nordic languages and the Ä or Ö in Finnish, Hungarian, Turkish and German.

Historically the letter A was pronounced in many different ways, just as it is in modern English with many variations such as warm, apple or darling. To make the spelling easier it was decided in Sweden in the 15th century to put an O above the A in cases where the pronunciation was that of warm, which created Å. In the next century came the addition of a little E over the A and O, to create Ä and Ö. But written signs have a tendency to transform its looks over the centuries and this elevated curly E was changed by lazy scribes or bad handwriting into the two dots you now find. The dots can also occasionally appear as a little straight line in hand-written documents.

TACK FÖR BESÖKET
VÄLKOMMEN ÅTER!

During the Viking Era the main language of Denmark, Sweden and Norway was Old Norse. Rune stones in the region were inscribed with letters known as "futhark" which is named after the first six characters of the runic alphabet. The pronunciation and spelling of Old Norse is not consistent with todays Nordic languages. One example is the old Æ which would sound like an Ä today, but if spoken by a Viking would sound like the longer tone of an A in the word 'after' in English, perhaps with an added nasal sound. The Vikings left plenty of words in Old Norse behind after their colonisation of the British Isles, including the names of the weekdays. The Nordic gods are represented in the names of four weekdays: Tuesday is named after the god of war Tyr, Wednesday after the main god Odin, Thursday after the god of thunder, Tor, and Friday is dedicated to Freya, the goddess of fertility. Modern Swedish certainly has its roots in Old Norse, but because of the many foreign influences on the language a Swede today would find communication with a Viking difficult. German words were added after traders and immigrant miners flooded into Sweden in the 15th century. In a few cases, English is more like Old Norse than the Swedish is. This explains why the English word "window" is derived from the Viking word "vindöga", (eye for the wind), whereas the Swedish word "fönster", is more like the German "Fenster".

Many thanks to the following persons and organisations who have helped us put this book together. Akvavit: The Absolut Company Blåbär: Vasaloppet Classic Cars: Göran Andell, motoring magazine Nostalgia * Conny Larsson, Sunnansjö, owner of a Chevvy Design: Peder Lamm, Nordéns Auctions * Ericsson (Cobra) * Hackman (Red Klara) * IKEA * Göran Bjarme (for lending us the Pernilla armchair) Emballage: MalacoLeaf Sverige * Cloetta Fazer * Kraft Sverige * Unilever * Abba Seafood * Tidernas Tennis, Båstad * Match Museum, Jönköping Fika: Doris Hemming Glas: Coca Cola * Orrefors Kosta Boda Haveri: The Vasa Museum Is: The Ice Hotel in Jukkasjärvi * Tomas Sarri, Same Radio * Jörgen Bäckström and Andreas Nutti, Nutti Sami Siida Jakt: Henrik Falk, Swedish Hunters Association * Alvar Johansson, Stimmerbo hunting team Lappland: Tomas Sarri, Same Radio Mammas Köttbullar: Ingemar Johansson and Edna Alsterlund-Johansson * Intersport Nobel: Nobel Organisation * Restaurant Stadshuskällaren Opera: Drottningholms Theatre museum and Royal Theatre Q-urbits: Dalarnas Museum * Ingemar and Barbro Lissmyr, Ludvika (for the interior pictures) * RST Kalktransporter, Rättvik * Ludvika Tourist Information Polska: Benny Andersson (for the image of the accordion) * Peter Carlsson & De Blå Grodorna * Kalle Moraeus * Björn Ranung, Peoples Museum in Stockholm * clothes consultant Kicki Kirwall-Hanses, Leksand Röd: Tommy Forss STORA-Enso * Museum of the Mine in Falun Traditioner: Mats Kärvås, Lions in Ludvika (for lending us the luciakrona) Uppfinningar: Håkan Lans Vikingar: The ship Svea Viking, Stockholm X: Rättviks Nature Museum * Dalhalla * Jämtland County Museum* The underground church St Anna in Kristineberg Zzz: Dr Urban Södergren, Stockholm

These books and websites were a great help: Akvavit: Steffo Törnquist, Hélène Tolstoy/ Sprit * Jan-Öjvind Swahn/ Mathistorisk uppslagsbok Blåbär: www.vasaloppet.se * Stig Hadenius, Torbjörn Nilsson, Gunnar Åselius/ Sveriges historia * Alf Henrikson/ Svensk historia Design: Jane Fredlund/ Stora boken om antikt Emballage: Jan-Öjvind Swahn/ Mathistorisk uppslagsbok * företagens hemsidor Fika: Lars Elgklou/ Kaffeboken Glas: Jan Brunius m fl / Svenskt glas * Jane Fredlund/ Stora boken om antikt Haveri: www.vasamuseet.se Is: www.jukkas.se Knäckebröd: Ria Wägner/ Läsebok för brödälskare Q-rbits: Chris Mosey & Michel Hjorth/ Dalahästar * www.nohemslojd.se Smörgåsbord: Steffo Törnquist, Hélène Tolstoy/ Sprit * Tore Wretman/ Smörgåsbordet Traditioner: www.spraknamnden.se Uppfinningar: ABB * Ron Kurtus, School for Champions * Lars Leander/ Tetra Pak * företagens hemsidor * www.si.se Vikingar: Bertil Almgren m fl/ Vikingen * Alf Henrikson/ Svensk historia X: Benny Kullinger/Rättviks naturmuseum/ Rättvik genom tiderna Yta: Microsoft Encarta * www.si.se <http://www.si.se/> . * www.orust.se * Bra Böckers lexikon Å, Ä, Ö: Bra Böckers lexikon * Lars Magnar Enoksen/ Runor * Alf Henrikson/ Svensk historia